"This is a book that every person should own, read and reread. It is filled with practical suggestions concerning how to help people grieving the death of a friend or relative. Every page rings true."

—Patton Boyle, Episcopal priest, pastoral counselor, author of *Screaming Hawk*

∽

"*As Much Time as it Takes* is sensitive, insightful, and practical to anyone who finds themselves wondering what to say, what to do, and what not to do in regard to a grieving friend or family member."

—Marina Maimer RN, St. Louis MS Hospice

∽

"This book tenderly touches every pain-swollen corner of a broken heart. This conversation incarnates the healing presence of God's grace...a gentle washing of the soul with hope, a telling of truth that restores the breath of faith."

—Reverend Helen W. Appelberg Founder of Compassionate Friends

~

"A lovely book."

—Joan Halifax, author of *Being with Dying*

~

As Much Time as it Takes is sensitive, insightful, and practical to anyone who finds themselves wondering what to say, what to do, and what not to do in regards to a grieving friend or family member."

—Marina Maimer RN, St. Louis MS Hospice

~

"This tenderly written book speaks to the heart of the process of accompanying loved ones through loss and bereavement. It is a much needed addition to an area rarely addressed in the literature dealing with grief and loss."

—Chris Ingenito, L.C.S.W., Hospice Care of Sonoma County

AS MUCH TIME AS IT TAKES

A GUIDE TO HEALTHY GRIEVING

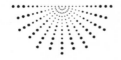

MARTIN KEOGH

INTIMATELY ROOTED BOOKS

AS MUCH TIME AS IT TAKES
A GUIDE TO HEALTHY GRIEVING
Copyright © 2018 Martin Keogh

Poem by Thomas Carlisle entitled "Our Jeopardy" © 1987 Theology Today. Originally published in issue 43 (1987): 559. Reprinted with the publisher's permission. Adapted by Jack Kornfield.

Excerpts from Gratefulness, the Heart of Prayer: An Approach to Life in Fullness by Brother David Steindl-Rast. Copyright © 1984 by David Steindl-Rast, Paulist Press, Inc. Used with permission of Paulist press. www.paulistpress.com.

The poems by Antonio Machado are translated by Robert Bly used with permission of the translator. (Times Alone. Middletown, Conn.: Wesleyan University Press, 1983)

Excerpt from "It Happened in Winter" from Extravagaria by Pablo Neruda, translated by Alastair Reid. Translation copyright © 1974 by Alastair Reid. Reprinted by permission of Farrar, Straus and Giroux, LLC.

- ISBN hardback: 978-1-7752430-5-2
- ISBN paperback: 978-1-7752430-6-9
- ISBN ebook: 978-1-7752430-7-6

Intimately Rooted Books
Salt Spring Island, BC Canada
For all of Martin Keogh's books visit:
martinkeogh.com

～

DEDICATION

*The friend who can be silent with us in
a moment of despair or confusion, who
can stay with us in an hour of grief or
bereavement, who can tolerate not
knowing, not curing, not healing and
face with us the reality of our
powerlessness, that is a friend
who cares.*

–Henri Nouwen, Out of Solitude

*To the memory of my parents
Linda and John
And my Soul friend
Grillo*

CONTENTS

INTRODUCTION

~

Do you know someone who recently lost a loved one? Do you wish to reach out to that person? This book is filled with practical and heartfelt ways to support people you care for who are grieving.

If you're grieving yourself, this book can help you recognize your own feelings and needs during this difficult and perhaps overwhelming time.

If you are a professional or volunteer, you will find a collection of tools and an empathy that result from placing yourself in the shoes of the bereaved.

The skills and rapport we need to support the bereaved are rarely taught to us at home or at school. Yet eventually we are all called on to have this knowledge, sometimes when we least expect it.

I began writing this guide shortly after losing

both my parents and a dear friend in quick succession. As I was grieving these deaths, I recognized that many people were uncomfortable being with me as I experienced such life-changing losses. I also realized many of the errors I made in the past while trying to console friends who were mourning.

A diverse group gave their time to this project. My profound appreciation goes to those who agreed to be interviewed and to all who offered feedback on the manuscript. These include hospice workers, grief therapists, midwives, priests, palliative care nurses, and many, many people who have recently had someone close to them die.

While this book addresses the family and friends of the bereaved, if someone close to *you* has died, these words can help you to acknowledge your feelings and needs during the different stages of your grieving and recovery process.

If you find yourself in the role of caregiver, listen to this book for the voice of *your* friend. When you turn the page and begin reading, imagine that these are words which he or she might be having trouble saying to you right now.

You can read this book in under an hour, yet the information and skills included here can help you to deepen your relationships throughout a lifetime. The appreciation for your caring and support can come back and touch you for years to come.

M.J.K.

PROLOGUE

My Dear Friend,

I have some terrible news. Somebody I cherish has died. I'm going through a difficult time right now, and I could use your support.

I realize that sometimes it's hard to know how to support someone who's grieving. One day they need company and the next day they need time alone. Sometimes, all they need is a friendly ear and sometimes the reminder to eat.

It's so easy to do or say something that can hurt a bereaved person that it's often challenging and confusing to know when and how to help. So, I've drawn this map for you, my friends. With all that's happened, it's difficult to ask for support. That's why I'm giving you this little guide.

Nothing in here takes a huge effort. I certainly don't want you to do anything that doesn't come from your love for me. In truth, most of the time, all I need is the small reminder that you care.

On the following pages, you will find many suggestions. Select the ones that feel right for you. You might be comfortable helping with practical matters, such as coordinating the funeral arrangements. Or you might wish to lend me an ear and give emotional support. This book is designed to help you discover what kinds of support feel most natural and effortless for you to offer.

You'll also find some activities and clichés to avoid during our times together. Your sensitivity to this information will encourage healing.

With death so close, each moment has become more precious. I'm grieving now, but I do want you to know I care for you. Thank you for being in my life and for all you've given.

With deep gratitude...

PART I
A FRAGILE CUP OF
REVELATION

Our Jeopardy

It is good to use best china
the most genuine goblets
the oldest lace tablecloth.
There's a risk, of course,
every time you use anything
or anyone shares an inmost moment,
or a fragile cup of revelation.
But not to touch, not to handle,
the artifacts of being human –
is the quiet crash, the deadly catastrophe

where nothing is enjoyed or broken
or spilled or spoken,
or stained, or mended –
where nothing is ever lived, loved,
laughed over, wept over,
where nothing is ever lost,
or found.

–Thomas Carlisle

CHAPTER ONE

Sometimes, I might feel embarrassed that I'm grieving and so vulnerable. I might become bewildered, not knowing how much I can reveal to you.

Sometimes, *you* might feel awkward, not knowing how to communicate with me while I'm grieving.

SOMETIMES IT'S GOING to feel downright clumsy for both of us.

AND THAT'S OKAY.

CHAPTER TWO

Often it feels
as though we need
a license
to make mistakes.

CHAPTER THREE

This grants
(insert name:)

_____

a bona fide license to
feel awkward
or uncomfortable
while in the unfamiliar territory
of the bereaved.

This license gives you permission
simply to be present
to the best of your ability.

PART II
IT SEEMS IMPOSSIBLE

FIRST AID FOR THE RECENTLY BEREAVED

I sat in the garden,
spattered by the great drops of winter,
and it seemed to me impossible
that beneath all that sadness,
that crumbled solitude,
the roots were still at work
with no one to encourage them.

–Pablo Neruda
(Translated by Alastair Reid)

CHAPTER FOUR

I've just learned of the death of my loved one.
    I don't want to be treated like someone
    who's infirm or bedridden.
    But sometimes, the smallest tasks
    feel overwhelming right now.

YOU MIGHT ASK:
    Is there anything I can do?

IN THIS STATE, I'm often not sure
    what I want or need.
    If I'm unable to answer you –
    and this is likely –
    please offer something specific.

CHAPTER FIVE

I want to help you understand
    what I'm going through.

SOMETIMES, it's overwhelming for me
    to live with this much emotion
    (or numbness).

YOU DON'T NEED to get overwhelmed as well.
    As you read the suggestions in these chapters,
    please remember you don't have to do
    everything.

These are choices.
If you're so moved,
select what feels natural for you.
These are the kindnesses
I'll appreciate most.   .

CHAPTER SIX

I'm emotionally exhausted.
    Sometimes, I'm forgetful.
    Small details seem overwhelming.

TELL me this is natural
    for someone who has just suffered
    this kind of loss.

CHAPTER SEVEN

If it feels like the right time,
    embrace me.
    And don't feel rejected
    if I shy away from physical contact.
    The touch might evoke emotions
    I'm not ready for right now.
    It's okay to try again later.

YOU MIGHT:

    • Hold my hand,

    • Wrap your arm around my shoulder,

    • Hug me tight. Let me rest my head on your shoulder.

CHAPTER EIGHT

Healing from an emotional injury
    can be similar
    to mending
    from a physical injury.

ENCOURAGE me to get enough sleep.
    Remind me to eat
    (unless you see me suppressing
    my feelings by overeating).

CHAPTER NINE

Feel free to bring over food,
    especially, homemade food
    that only needs to be heated and served.
    I especially have a hankering
    for comfort foods:

- Homemade chicken soup
- Macaroni and cheese
- Warm tapioca
- Mashed potatoes
- Anything creamy

Ask me about my personal favorites.
The foods I enjoyed while growing up
may be indigenous to other cultures.
Or I may have special dietary needs.

CHAPTER TEN

I'm having trouble
   telling people about my loss.
   On top of my own tidal waves
   of emotion (or numbness),
   I have to deal with
   other people's reactions
   and discomfort.

YOU COULD HELP
   by offering to make phone calls
   so I don't need to be the first
   to tell people the news.

CHAPTER ELEVEN

You might offer
    to sleep over,
    so I don't feel isolated
    (especially if I live alone).

Or, if it works for you,
    tell me I can call you anytime –
    day or night.

CHAPTER TWELVE

If I have children,
    offer to spend time with them.
    I might need someone responsible
    to take care of them,
    until I am better able to function.
    I may need to rest and grieve alone,
    knowing my children
    are in safe hands.

BUT PLEASE UNDERSTAND,
    if one of my children has died,
    I might not want anybody else
    to take care of my surviving children
    for a while.

CHAPTER THIRTEEN

See if I've taken care of business.
    Ask me if I've paid my utility bills
    or if I have any other pressing
    financial obligations to handle.
    Have I let them know at work
    that I won't be coming in?

Do I have appointments
    that need to be changed or canceled?
    You might offer to handle
    some of my paperwork
    or return phone calls.

CHAPTER FOURTEEN

I can feel overwhelmed
by having to take care of so many details.
If you're skillful at making arrangements,
you might offer to help
with some of these tasks:

- Making plans with the funeral home
- Arranging for the death certificate
- Inviting people to the funeral
- Helping to greet people and keeping a list of all who attend or call
- Arranging transportation and housing for people from out of town
- Helping me with correspondence and thank you notes

CHAPTER FIFTEEN

Or perhaps you could offer to help with:

- Shopping for groceries
- Mowing the lawn
- Walking the dog
- Doing the laundry
- Driving me to appointments
- The gardening and household tasks

CHAPTER SIXTEEN

Marking this passage by a memorial
    or tribute to celebrate the person's life
    can be an important part
    of the grieving process.
    It allows me to more fully realize
    the person is gone
    and gives me the opportunity
    to say good-bye.

PLEASE RESPECT my religious
    or spiritual traditions
    and those of family and friends
    during the funeral
    and the mourning period.

CHAPTER SEVENTEEN

If we are at a loss
   for ideas for the service,
   you could gently suggest we:

- Encourage people to share stories about the person
- Read letters from friends and family and the person who has died
- Don't exclude telling jokes and tenderly "roasting" the person
- Sing his favorite songs
- Play videos and audios and make available personal mementos, letters, and photographs

PART III
AS MUCH TIME AS IT TAKES

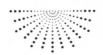

*The heart is a leisurely muscle. It differs
from all other muscles. How many
push-ups can you make before the
muscles in your arms and stomach get
so tired that you have to stop? But your
heart muscle goes on working for as
long as you live. It does not get tired,
because there is a phase of rest built
into every single heartbeat. Our
physical heart works leisurely.*

*And when we speak of the heart in a wider
sense, the idea that life-giving leisure
lies at the very center is implied. Never*

*to lose sight of that central place of
leisure in our life would keep us
youthful. Seen in this light, leisure is
not a privilege but a virtue. Leisure is
not the privilege of a few who can
afford to take time, but the virtue of all
who are willing to give time to what
takes time – to give as much time as a
task rightly takes.*

–Brother David Steindl-Rast

CHAPTER EIGHTEEN

In my grandparents' day,
    there was more support for grieving.
    Many generations of the family
    gathered together.
    People wore black for a time
    after a person's death.
    Often, there were wakes in the home.
    Now, I'm expected back at work in a few days.
    People expect me to be "fully functional."
    The small reminder that I'm grieving
    and may need to slow down
    and heal goes a long way.
    Encourage me to go at my own pace.
    Keep reminding me of the importance of
    putting my own needs before
    other people's expectations.

CHAPTER NINETEEN

It's often too easy for me to
    get caught up
    in other people's rhythms and needs.
    You might see people smothering me
    with an excess of well-intentioned kindness.

PLEASE PLAY "INTERFERENCE" for me.
    If some *yakkety-yak* comes up
    and starts overwhelming me
    with chatter,
    come and engage them,
    so I can slip away.

CHAPTER TWENTY

Encourage me
   not to make
   any big decisions
   for a while.

A BIG ENOUGH
   life change
   has already
   taken place.

CHAPTER TWENTY-ONE

I have so much going on inside
    that when you're with me
    you don't need to do much.
    I probably feel most comfortable
    when you give off a calm,
    relaxed air that leads me to feel:

- There's plenty of time
- There's no rush
- I can take the space I need to feel what
  needs to be felt

When we're together,
make it easy for yourself:
Most times, you don't have to *do* anything.
Just your presence makes me feel better.

CHAPTER TWENTY-TWO

If it seems I'm keeping myself
    unusually busy...
    If you see me running around
    most of the time...
    If I'm numb...
    If I'm having trouble crying...
    Invite me over
    for a lazy afternoon or evening
    where we don't do much.
    Offer to run me a bath,
    or we can watch a sad movie,
    or listen to some sad music.*

_____

*Some people who have suffered a big loss
discover a sudden and mysterious appreciation for
Country & Western music!

CHAPTER TWENTY-THREE

Come and hang out in my home –
    maybe not even in the same room.

We can sit and read together.
    Cook a meal.
    Talk in candlelight.

Nothing special.

And let's keep the TV and other screens off.

CHAPTER TWENTY-FOUR

At times,
   I may simply need
   the house to myself
   or an afternoon to walk alone
   in the woods.

HELP me preserve
   some intervals for solitude.

ENCOURAGE me
   to put aside times
   in my calendar
   for dates with myself.

CHAPTER TWENTY-FIVE

Take me out into nature.
  The majesty of nature
  can help bring comfort
  and take me to that deep
  wordless place
  where I can see my loss
  from a larger perspective.

INVITE ME TO:
  • Walk barefoot on the beach
  • Absorb the stillness and silence of a desert
  • Watch a sunset from high up on the edge of a
canyon
  • Lie down and gaze at the Milky Way

CHAPTER TWENTY-SIX

Please don't try to save me
    from my feelings.
    By truly going through
    all the feelings that arise
    with losing a dear one,
    I'm being brought more deeply
    into my life.
    I'm also being asked
    to look squarely
    into the face
    of my own death.

CHAPTER TWENTY-SEVEN

From a spiritual point of view,
    this can be an important
    time for me.

GENTLY ENCOURAGE me
    to take my time
    with every aspect
    of this process and
    to live each stage fully.

PART IV
A GENTLE AND TENDER HAND

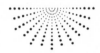

*When we honestly ask ourselves which
person in our lives means the most to
us, we often find that it is those who,
instead of giving much advice,
solutions, or cures, have chosen rather
to share our pain and touch our
wounds with a gentle and tender hand.*

–Henri Nouwen, *Out of Solitude*

CHAPTER TWENTY-EIGHT

I might feel reserved and insecure
    when you first visit or call.
    I may not be sure of your intentions.

PLEASE TRY NOT to arrive
    with some big plan.
    The first important step for me
    is to establish an unafraid,
    heartfelt communication.

CHAPTER TWENTY-NINE

Look for my cues; let me lead.
    I may not know what I want,
    but I'm quickly aware
    of what I don't want;
    please look for signs of my resistance
    and respect them.

WHEN YOU MAKE AN OFFER,
    always give me the option
    of something else,
    or of nothing at all.

SOME DAYS, I don't want to *do* anything.

CHAPTER THIRTY

If you're having trouble
    picking up my cues, try this:
    Take a moment and imagine yourself
    in my place.

IMAGINE you've had this loss
    and what you might be feeling.
    Imagine what you might need
    from those around you.
    You may find you simply desire
    love and acceptance.

CHAPTER THIRTY-ONE

In your own way,
    tell me that you love me.
    And why.

TALK to me
    about my strengths.
    Remind me
    of my good qualities.

CHAPTER THIRTY-TWO

Send me messages, texts
    or emails. Better yet, send something
    tangible like cards or flowers.
    Remind me that you care.
    Write me a love letter.
    Tell me what you remember
    about the person who has died.

SOMETIMES, it just takes
    too much effort for me
    to telephone you.
    Call me regularly and leave messages
    (and remind me I don't need
    to return your calls).
    If you feel like you might be
    calling too much: ask me.

CHAPTER THIRTY-THREE

Find out when it's hardest for me.
    Quite likely,
    it is Saturday evenings
    or Sundays.

INVITE ME OVER.
    Ask me what I'd like to do
    and if I'd like anyone else to join us.

CHAPTER THIRTY-FOUR

With so much going on,
   I might be forgetting my body.
   Encourage me to get exercise.

JOIN me in some quiet stretching
   to bring me *home*.
   Or join me in some activities
   that get my body moving,
   my blood pumping,
   and my sweat flowing.

CHAPTER THIRTY-FIVE

Offer to massage my feet
or hands.
Rub my shoulders.
Ask if I would like a full massage
from you or from a professional.
Offer to arrange the appointment for me
if I keep putting it off.

CHAPTER THIRTY-SIX

My sex drive might drop
   for a while.
   Or it may go up.
   If we have a sexual relationship,
   please be sensitive.

OPENING up sexually
   at this time
   may make me feel especially vulnerable.
   I may cry when we make love.

CHAPTER THIRTY-SEVEN

Help me to surround myself
   with beauty.

SUPPORT me in keeping my personal
   environment peaceful and harmonious.

   - Ask me what colors I feel good wearing.
   - Fill my kitchen with flowers.
   - Find out if I'd like to go a museum, an art
     gallery, or a sculpture garden.
   - Find out what music I like and play it
     while you're with me.

CHAPTER THIRTY-EIGHT

Create a ritual with me.

IT CAN BE SIMPLE. We can:

- Light a candle by the deceased's photo
- Sing his favorite songs
- Tell stories of when she was most: sweet, courageous, rotten, funny
- Write, draw, or dance our feelings about this loss
- Call out his name
- Chant, pray, or meditate together
- Visit the cemetery or disperse the ashes together

CHAPTER THIRTY-NINE

You're giving a lot to me right now. Please remember: *Take care of yourself.*

KNOW YOUR LIMITS.
Don't overextend yourself.
If you're deeply uncomfortable
around tears or anger, let me know this
and excuse yourself when I cry or rage.

TALK to your friends about any
confusion or anxiety you feel with me.

Take time away when you need it –
in the next room, out in the countryside,
or any way that works best for you.

PART V
GIVING SORROW WORDS

Give sorrow words; the grief that does
  not speak
Whispers the o'er-fraught heart, and bids
  it break.

–Shakespeare

CHAPTER FORTY

I'm trying to understand
   what has come crashing
   into my life.
   By wrapping words
   around my experience
   and my feelings,
   I'm attempting to make sense
   of a life that is
   now vastly different.

MAY I TALK TO YOU?

CAN I tell you my stories?

CHAPTER FORTY-ONE

I don't know how to describe
    what's going on inside me.
    But I may need to try.
    And it will take a while.

ASK ME,
    "How are you doing?"
    when you have the time
    and receptivity
    to hear the answer.

CHAPTER FORTY-TWO

Sometimes I might get stuck
   trying to be "appropriate"
   or trying to please you.
   As we talk, it helps me
   when I feel there's nowhere else
   in the world you'd rather be.

REMIND me that I don't need
   to entertain you
   or take care of you.
   And if you can,
   listen to what I say
   with a calm and open silence.

CHAPTER FORTY-THREE

Place yourself,
   sitting,
   standing
   or lying down,
   at the same level
   as I am.
   Let your body be open,
   your arms and legs
   uncrossed.
   Let yourself be relaxed.
   Don't be afraid
   of eye contact
   (and don't force it).
   If it feels right,
   touch me.

It helps if you use little cues
    to let me know
    you're listening.
    Words, phrases
    and questions like:

- Really?
- Um, uh-huh, and oh!
- How did that make you feel?
- That's awful...
- What happened next?

These tell me
you're listening
and interested.

Questions that call for "yes" or "no" answers can
make me uncomfortable:

- Were you happy together?
- Are you hurting?
- Were you satisfied with the funeral?

BECAUSE ONCE I'VE ANSWERED "YES" or "no,"
I often don't know what to say next.

INSTEAD, use open-ended phrases and questions like:

- How did you meet...?

- Could you tell me about the time you...?
- I can't imagine how hard this is for you...
- What was it like at the end...?
- Tell me one of your favorite memories...

THESE ENCOURAGE ME TO TALK.

CHAPTER FORTY-SIX

Don't pull me out of my feelings
    with small talk.
    I don't need to be distracted
    from my grief right now.

BUT you also don't need
    to put on an air of false solemnity.
    In fact, sometimes a sense of humor
    is just what's needed.
    Humor used skillfully
    often helps to bring some movement,
    some levity,
    and a deepening of emotion.

CHAPTER FORTY-SEVEN

On my lead,
    bring in some gallows humor.
    And don't be shocked
    when I make jokes
    about the dead...

SOMETIMES,
    the most healing activity
    is to laugh at death.*

---

*A man in a bereavement group who had been married for 52 years was about to take his wife's ashes through customs. He was trying to imagine what he would say if a customs official tried to open the urn. "If he sticks his hand in the urn, I'm going to have to tell him, 'Get your hand off my wife's ash!'"

CHAPTER FORTY-EIGHT

Don't be surprised
    when I surround myself
    with photos of the person who died...
    Or when I wear her shirt to bed...
    Or when I go to the places
    we visited together...
    Or when I do anything else
    that helps bring the memories to life.

CHAPTER FORTY-NINE

Reminisce with me.
    Tell me stories
    about the one I've lost.
    Bring him closer
    by invoking his memory.
    Allow me to tell the stories
    of our relationship –
    of the pleasures and betrayals,
    of our adventures and misadventures.
    And allow me to tell you about the hole
    I feel in my heart.

Try not to philosophize
    or strive to make me feel better.
    This devalues my feelings of loss
    and makes me feel wrong for my pain.

CHAPTER FIFTY

I'm probably not ready
  to hear expressions like these:

- Everything will be okay...
- She'll always be with you...
- Good thing he's out of pain...
- I'm sure she's looking down on us from
  heaven now...
- You're lucky you had so much time
  together...
- Someday, you'll look back at this and...

When I hear phrases that attempt
to counteract what I'm feeling,
I sometimes get confused or upset.
I'm grieving, and the emotions
I'm feeling are part of the healing process.

CHAPTER FIFTY-ONE

More clichés to avoid:

- You must be strong (for the family/for the children etc.).
- I know she wouldn't want you to cry.
- Well, life goes on.
- God will never give you more than you can handle.
- You should count your blessings (or any other "should").
- Now you can get on with your life.
- He's with God now.

CHAPTER FIFTY-TWO

Please don't try
to solve my "problems."
Stay away from giving advice.*
If I ask you for advice,
you might first ask me,
"What do *you* think?"
Or: "How do *you* feel about it?"
And please don't preach.

JUST BE BY MY SIDE –
an equal, a human being,
a friend.

————————————

*If you feel compelled to give advice, advise me to accept offers of help from my friends. I'm probably having some difficulty with this.

CHAPTER FIFTY-THREE

If we're both bereaved,
    we can be an invaluable resource
    for each other
    during this difficult time.
    Our ears can be wide open
    with compassion.
    Let's allow each other
    to have our own timing
    and individual styles of grieving,
    even though we might be suffering
    a similar loss.

CHAPTER FIFTY-FOUR

Don't be afraid
    to speak the name
    of the deceased.

THIS IS WORTH REPEATING:

DON'T BE afraid
    to speak the name
    of the deceased.

CHAPTER FIFTY-FIVE

∼

Don't feel the need...

to fill...

...the silences.

CHAPTER FIFTY-EIGHT

After some silence,
 I might want to say:
 "You're giving me a lot right now.
 Sometimes it's hard
 to let you know,
 but I'm extremely grateful
 for your kindness."

PART VI
MY HEART AND THE SEA

Lord, you have ripped away from me what
    I loved most.
One more time, O God, hear me cry out
    inside.
"Your will be done," it was done, and
    mine not.
My heart and the sea are together, Lord,
    and alone.

–Antonio Machado
(Translated by Robert Bly)

CHAPTER FIFTY-NINE

Tears are nature's balm
for emotional injuries.
Your permission for me to cry
is one of the most loving things
you can give me right now.
If I cry, I'm revealing the confidence
I have in you.
I trust you enough
to show you my vulnerability.
Remember that I won't cry forever
(and that crying sometimes
leads to laughter).

CHAPTER SIXTY

It's okay to cry with me.
  However, don't *expect* me to cry.
  Sometimes, my tears are spent,
  or I might be someone
  who doesn't cry around others.
  You might simply hear me sigh
  instead of crying.

IF YOU CAN'T TAKE my tears,
  if they make you too upset
  or confused, let me know.
  We'll work something out.

CHAPTER SIXTY-ONE

From moment to moment,
    different voices will rise up in me:

- I didn't appreciate him enough.
- I hate her for dying.
- If only I had...
- It's all my fault.
- It's all his fault.
- I'm overwhelmed, it's too much, I'm afraid.
- I'll never love again.

THESE VOICES ARE ACCOMPANIED
    by strong emotions.
    If I trust you enough to speak them

in your presence,
please don't invalidate them.
Don't respond with phrases like:
"Oh no, that's not true; you'll be fine,"
or "You did all you could,"
or "Of course you'll love again."

ACKNOWLEDGE THIS IS
what I'm feeling at this time.
Recognize that it must be hard for me,
rather than telling me
that what I'm feeling
is not true
or that it will be different
someday soon.

CHAPTER SIXTY-TWO

Let me have my feelings now.
    Perspective can come later.

CHAPTER SIXTY-THREE

I want to tell you
    about our last days together,
    about how we met.
    I want to tell you I feel bad
    that I didn't appreciate him enough
    while he was alive.

I WANT to show you her picture
    and tell you about the plans we had...

...THAT SHE TREATED ME BADLY,
    gave me lots of gifts,
    was unbearably ornery.

I WANT to tell you I feel guilty
    that a part of me is relieved
    he's dead.

I WANT TO WAIL, WHY?
    Where is she?
    How could this happen?
    How can God do such a thing?
    I want to shout,

NO! IT CAN'T BE TRUE!

CHAPTER SIXTY-FOUR

If I get emotional
 and the words are not coming easily,
 you can reassure me
 with phrases such as,
 "Take your time."
 "It's okay."

Allow me to do most of the talking.
 Feel free to ask questions,
 but have your own responses as well,
 so it doesn't become an interrogation.
 Once I open up,
 please don't change the subject.
 If you're getting overwhelmed,
 let me know.

CHAPTER SIXTY-FIVE

People often say to me,
    "I understand."
    This can make me angry.
    Not even I can fathom
    the depths of my feelings right now.
    How can anyone else say
    they understand
    what I'm feeling?

OFTEN, it's better to say:

- I can't imagine what you're going through...
- I'm here with you...
- Tell me about it...
- It doesn't feel fair...
- I'll stay close by, so you can find me when you are ready...

CHAPTER SIXTY-SIX

Hearing my stories might remind you
   of your own losses and sorrows.

SHARE THEM.

WHEN I HEAR ABOUT similar stories
   and feelings,
   it helps me to feel like I'm not crazy,
   despite all that's going on inside me.

BUT PLEASE BE BRIEF,
   so that I don't get pulled out
   of my emotions.

CHAPTER SIXTY-SEVEN

Sometimes, you might find me
  quite angry,
  especially if I have suffered
  a sudden loss.

- I'll rage at the drunk driver.
- Call the doctors "incompetent buffoons."
- Lash out at my friends who "don't understand."

If you can,
stay with me;
let me feel my anger.
This too will pass.

CHAPTER SIXTY-EIGHT

If I'm raging,
    offer to accompany me
    to the railroad tracks,
    so that I can scream
    as loud as I can
    as the train passes by.
    This also works
    by the ocean.
    It's big enough
    to absorb all my anger.

CHAPTER SIXTY-NINE

If you're feeling strong,
 stand beside me
 as I curse God
 for the injustice!
 For the loss!
 For this death!
 God doesn't need
 your defense.
 Sometimes, what's felt inside
 has to be said aloud
 (very a-loud)
 to be released.

CHAPTER SEVENTY

Sometimes, I'm going to be intense,
    sometimes irrational
    and sometimes numb.
    At times, it's not going to be easy
    to be at my side.
    But remember,
    I'm glad you're with me
    as I go through this.
    I *need* you here.
    And I appreciate your willingness
    to be at my side
    even through the discomfort.

CHAPTER SEVENTY-ONE

And remember to be sensitive
    to your own feelings.

If you're uneasy
    around my anger,
    say, "I'm uncomfortable,"
    rather than trying to distract me
    by changing the subject.

If you feel anxiety or fear,
    you don't need to pretend
    it's not there. Tell me.

This honesty will bring us closer together.

CHAPTER SEVENTY-TWO

I welcome your feelings...

...BUT PLEASE DON'T GET SO
emotionally distraught
that I end up
jumping out of myself
to take care of you.

CHAPTER SEVENTY-THREE

In the end, what you say
  or do is not what's most important.
  Your attempts to open up to me,
  to be with me in a vulnerable,
  sometimes uncomfortable,
  and compassionate place in your heart
  will likely be healing for *both* of us.

IT MIGHT TAKE MORE energy
  than you imagined
  to be with me through these dark days.
  But it can create a deep bond
  of friendship between us.

PART VII
BONE BY BONE

There is a pain so utter –
It swallows substance up –
Then covers the Abyss with Trance –
So Memory can step
Around-across-upon it –
As one within a Swoon –
Goes safely – where an open eye –
Would drop Him – Bone by Bone

–Emily Dickinson

People often make
    a hierarchy of dying.
    They might feel it's better
    to die of heart failure than from cancer –
    it's better to die of cancer than AIDS –
    it's better to die of AIDS than suicide.
    Please don't let your judgments
    affect your compassion for my loss.

People need to grieve many kinds of death.
 Perhaps I have lost someone to:

- violent crime
- a birth defect
- a trauma such as a car or plane accident

Or maybe I have lost:

- an adult child
- a spouse who has been in pain for years
- a friend whose death is unexplainable

Your sensitivity and ability to improvise
with the particular loss
I'm suffering
is welcome.

CHAPTER SEVENTY-SIX

If I've lost a child,
    I'm in a particularly sensitive place.
    We're not made to live through such a loss.
    We're not supposed to bury our children.
    This kind of loss feels different
    than any other.

PLEASE DON'T COMPARE my loss
    to the loss of a parent,
    a spouse,
    or a pet.

CHAPTER SEVENTY-SEVEN

Know that I may be no less crushed
   by the loss of an unborn child
   to miscarriage or abortion.

I MIGHT BE FEELING a profound emptiness
   at the loss of the *person* to be,
   and the loss of my unfulfilled dreams
   for *my* baby.

CHAPTER SEVENTY-EIGHT

Some clichés to avoid
   around the death of a child:

- God wanted another flower for his garden.
- Well, you still have_____.
- At least it was now and not when he was older and you were even more attached.
- God wanted another angel.
- You can still have another child.

CHAPTER SEVENTY-NINE

If you can, be there
    for my children and their grief.
    Just like the time you spend with me,
    listen to my children
    with wide-open ears.
    It's important
    not to use euphemisms
    such as "gone away,"
    "left us," or "is sleeping."
    These can be misinterpreted
    and cause the child anxiety.

LET my children know
    my emotions of grief or anger
    or withdrawal are about
    the person who died.

REASSURE my children
    they are not responsible
    for these feelings:
    "He's not sad because of
    anything you did;
    he's crying because he's unhappy
    that your grandfather died last week."

TOGETHER, you can create
    little rituals of good-bye –
    draw a picture, write a letter,
    or blow out a candle
    for the one who has died.

CHAPTER EIGHTY

If I've lost someone to suicide,
    I may feel guilt, regret,
    and a profound sense of abandonment.
    It may be especially hard
    for me to talk about
    what has happened.
    Encourage me to talk about the gifts
    and pains of the person's *entire* life
    and death.

CHAPTER EIGHTY-ONE

If you consistently hear me say
    things like, "I'd be better off dead,"
    ask me if I'm thinking about suicide.
    If I say "yes," ask me if I have a plan.
    If I say "yes," direct me right away to a

- Therapist
- Spiritual counselor
- Member of the clergy
- Suicide prevention line

And make sure there are people
to keep me company at all times.

CHAPTER EIGHTY-TWO

If you see me retreating
    into excesses of alcohol, drugs,
    or time online:
    offer similar support.

IF I OWN a gun
    and you see
    I'm extremely distressed,
    offer to take care of it for a while.

AND TELL me I really am
    important to you
    and that you'd never want to see
    any harm come to me.

CHAPTER EIGHTY-THREE

Put me in touch with individuals or groups
    who have survived a similar loss.

You can locate information about bereavement
    support groups online or through a local hospice
or hospital.

If I've lost a child, get in touch with a
    Compassionate Friends group
    and have one of their members contact me:
    www.compassionatefriends.org

Please don't pressure me into joining a group,
    but you might offer to drive me to a meeting.

PART VIII
WATER OF A NEW LIFE

Last night, as I was sleeping,
I dreamt – marvelous error!
that a spring was breaking
out in my heart.
I said: along which secret aqueduct,
Oh water, are you coming to me,
water of a new life
that I have never drunk?

Last night, as I was sleeping,
I dreamt – marvelous error!
that I had a beehive
here inside my heart.
And the golden bees

were making white combs
and sweet honey
from my old failures.

Last night, as I was sleeping,
I dreamt – marvelous error!
that a fiery sun was giving
light inside my heart.
It was fiery because I felt
warmth as from a hearth,
and sun because it gave light
and brought tears to my eyes.

Last night, as I was sleeping,
I dreamt – marvelous error!
that it was God I had here inside my heart.

–Antonio Machado
(Translated by Robert Bly)

CHAPTER EIGHTY-FOUR

Now that some time has passed,
    I have more vitality.
    I can see signs of life everywhere.
    This death will be a part of me always,
    but I'm beginning to remember
    the person with more feelings of love
    than loss.
    The world is a more inviting place.
    I have more energy
    for giving to others and to you.
    Life all around me
    (and in me)
    is perking up!

CHAPTER EIGHTY-FIVE

There comes a time
  when structure can be helpful.

ENCOURAGE me
  to put some things
  in my schedule.
  Join me hiking, swimming,
  playing tennis, or at a concert.
  Remind me of my hobbies.

GET me involved in some projects –
  especially projects where I get to help others
  who are less fortunate than me.

CHAPTER EIGHTY-SIX

Bring over animals
    and children
    and plants
    to keep me company
    and to remind me
    of life.

CHAPTER EIGHTY-SEVEN

Keep sending cards,
  even when it appears
  that everything is back
  to "normal."

IN TIME you can send greetings
  without referring to the loss.

CHAPTER EIGHTY-EIGHT

Please don't assume
    I have finished grieving –
    weeks, months, or even years later.

YOUR SUPPORT and love
    are always welcome...

...HOWEVER, if after a long time,
    my life appears *paralyzed*
    in grieving,
    encourage me
    to work with a counselor
    or a bereavement group.

CHAPTER EIGHTY-NINE

One of the kindest things
    you can do is call
    or spend time with me
    during and just before and after
    the hard days:

- birthdays: his and mine
- holidays
- the anniversaries of her death

CHAPTER NINETY

Why don't you and I
    go out and have some fun?
    Invite me to socialize,
    perhaps starting with small groups
    and working up from there.
    Invite me
    to reconnect with old friends
    and meet new people.
    Offer to accompany me
    as I head out into the world again.
    I may need a companion
    for driving to work,
    attending church,
    spending a day at the beach...

CHAPTER NINETY-ONE

It's time for some pampering.

Suggest something nourishing
  (or even indulgent!)
  that I might not normally do:

- Dining at a fine restaurant
- Getting a facial, pedicure, or manicure
- Shopping for something special
- Soaking at a hot springs together
- Milk shakes, sundaes, ice cream!

CHAPTER NINETY-TWO

I'm more sensitive and perceptive
    because of the range of emotions
    I've been living with.
    Inside, I'm opened up
    in new and stimulating ways
    to people, to nature, and to the world.

Now that I'm grieving less,
    I have more energy.
    This combination of increased energy
    and heightened sensitivity
    makes this an ideal time for creativity.
    Encourage me to get involved
    in artistic and creative pursuits.
    Join me if you share my interests.

CHAPTER NINETY-THREE

You know it's been a rough road for me.
    Sometimes, I've wondered
    if I would make it through.
    But with your presence,
    your help,
    and your willingness to listen,
    every day I feel a little more alive.

I *AM* MAKING IT THROUGH,
    and you deserve a lot of recognition
    for *your* kindness
    and generous support.

PART IX
EPILOGUE

CHAPTER NINETY-FOUR

This guide is almost finished,
    but not quite...
    You get to complete it yourself.

REMEMBER you have a particular way
    you demonstrate your caring.
    Take these suggestions
    as a framework
    and then express yourself
    in the style that's natural for you.

CHAPTER NINETY-FIVE

You can trust yourself.

CHAPTER NINETY-SIX

Sometimes, when we're asked to help,
    we're called on to expand
    how we see ourselves as human beings.
    By helping me with this loss,
    you might have found
    yourself changed.

MY GRATITUDE RUNS deep
    for your willingness
    to take this risk.

MY DEAR FRIEND,

My Dear Friend,
How can I tell you how important
your support has been?

YOU'VE BEEN by my side through an
extremely difficult period. Your caring
and compassion have truly helped me heal
and grow into living my life more fully.

I WILL NEVER FORGET we've shared
some of the most vulnerable and intimate
times that people can experience together.

THANK YOU. I want to tell you: I love you.

~

ACKNOWLEDGMENTS

This book is dedicated to my parents and to Grillo.

My mother, Linda, was a passionate artist who cherished being the center of attention. She loved to cook, to eat, to create, and to receive praise. My father, John, was a life-long athlete, and a dignified and reserved man. He had a sense of humor that held no punches, and a great fondness for language and leisure. My friend Grillo loved people – and people loved her. She could disarm a bureaucrat, a mean-ass biker, or a close friend with her presence and smile.

I've written this book as a tribute to the vitality and love these three exuded and to the important roles they played in so many people's lives including my own.

~

This book would not exist if it were not for Kristelle Sim. Her unwavering support, straightforward feedback, and ability to get the manuscript to the right individuals is why this book is now in your hands. My editor, Elianne Obadia, helped give this book its form and poetry – she truly is the Writer's Midwife.

The following friends had the generosity to not be shy in their feedback: Robert Bly, Byron Brown, Dharamkaur Sing Khalsa, Liz Rozner, Mary Ford, and Owen Jones.

Many people read the manuscript in the early stages and gave their comments. I'll mention them here, along with those friends whose steadfast belief in the book kept me writing: Anne Aronov, Anne Kilcoyne, Chris Ingenito, Clover Catskill, Cynthia Sterling, Dawn Banghart, Dorie Beach, Elizabeth Alach, Gretchen Spiro, Helena Worthen, Jillaine Smith, Karen Roeper, Kate Murdoch, Ken and Barbara Luboff, Kirk Andrews, Leigh Hollowgrass, Loie Rosencrantz, Marion and Russ Archibald, Mary Herzog, Michael Steinberg, Nina Keogh, Pakina Fernandez, Paulina Hawkins, Peter Rosselli, Ray Landes, Rita Krug, Tony Jerez, and Wendy Fox.

And for the spark of life, I'm grateful to my wife and companion, Liza Keogh.

ABOUT THE AUTHOR

Martin Keogh founded *The Dancing Ground,* an orga-
nization that offers conferences and symposia on
gender, race, and mythology. He has produced and
taught with the likes of Joseph Campbell, Robert Bly,
Clarissa Pinkola Estés, Coleman Barks, and James
Hillman.

After attending Stanford University, Martin
hitchhiked 25,000 miles through North America and
spent time traveling to monasteries in Japan and
Korea. In 1979, he became a Dharma Teacher and
director of the Empty Gate Zen Center in Berkeley,
California.

Martin was named a Fulbright Senior Specialist
for his contribution to the development of the inter-
personal partner dance form, Contact Improvisa-

tion. For nearly four decades, he has led master classes, teacher conferences, and intensive trainings in 32 countries spanning six continents.

Martin's writings have appeared in nine languages. He is author of Dancing Deeper Still (Intimately Rooted Books, 2018) and the editor of Hope Beneath Our Feet: Restoring Our Place in the Natural World (North Atlantic Books, 2010).

After the loss of three loved ones in close succession, Martin gathered information from professionals in the bereavement field, including palliative care nurses, hospice workers, priests, and grief therapists. This information is synthesized in *As Much Time as it Takes.*

Martin lives with his family on the shores of the Salish Sea in British Columbia.

More information at: www.martinkeogh.com

Made in the USA
Monee, IL
10 December 2020

51724738R00090